# Steamers of Loch Lomond
## *by* P. J. G. Ransom

C000297118

The *Prince Edward*, on her southbound run, at Inversnaid Pier.

# A Splendid Motor Run from Glasgow

## Or Travel via BALLOCH (N.B.R. or C.R.) or via CRAIGENDORAN and WEST HIGHLAND RAILWAY to ARROCHAR & TARBET Station

*The* **Tarbet Hotel**

• *LOCH LOMOND* •

MOUNTAINEERING
TROUT and SALMON
FISHING ~ BOATING
GOLFING ~ TENNIS
Splendid Roads for
MOTORING & CYCLING

Principal Hotel on the Loch ~ in the
Centre of the Grandest Highland Scenery

Text © P. J. G. Ransom, 2007.
First published in the United Kingdom, 2007,
by Stenlake Publishing Ltd.
www.stenlake.co.uk
ISBN 978-1-84033-396-1

The publishers regret that they cannot supply
copies of any pictures featured in this book.

## Further Reading

Alan Brown, *Loch Lomond Passenger Steamers 1818-1989*, Allan T. Condie
    Publications, Nuneaton, 2000.
C.L.D. Duckworth & G.E. Langmuir, *Clyde River and Other Steamers*,
    Brown, Son & Ferguson Ltd, Glasgow, 1972.
D. Graham, *Sunset on the Clyde*, Neil Wilson Publishing, Glasgow, 1993.
P.J.G. Ransom, *Loch Lomond and the Trossachs in History and Legend*,
    John Donald Publishers, Edinburgh, 2004.

None of these books are available from Stenlake Publishing; please contact your local
bookshop or reference library.

## Acknowledgements

I am most grateful for information kindly provided by Brian Hillsdon, archivist of the
Steam Boat Association of Great Britain. My wife and my agent, Duncan McAra, have
been as supportive as ever.

Despite the heading, the illustration on this Tarbet Hotel publicity material
emphasises the hotel's convenient proximity to the steamer pier. The same artwork
was used by the Caledonian Railway for a full-colour poster to encourage people to
come by train and steamer – so it does seem a little ungracious for the hotel to use it
to promote travel by motor car!

# INTRODUCTION

The first steamer to go into service on Loch Lomond was David Napier's *Marion* in 1818. That was only eleven years after Fulton had started the world's first successful steamer service on the Hudson River, and six years after Bell did the same for Europe with his *Comet* on the Clyde. One of the first people to describe the *Marion* was Francis Jeffray, noted lawyer and political commentator, who spent holidays at Tarbet and Stuckgown. He observed the vessel 'hissing and roaring … foaming and shouting like an angry whale'. He added, 'I am glad it has been found not to answer, and is to be dropped next year'. He could scarcely have been more wrong. From 1818 there were paddle steamers in operation on Loch Lomond continuously until 1981, an astonishing record. In that year the last of them, the *Maid of the Loch*, took her last cruise. Restoration by her present owner, the charitable Loch Lomond Steamship Company, is already far advanced and the day when she once again steams up and down the loch is probably not far off.

Like steamers, tourists started to come to Loch Lomond in the early nineteenth century and it was largely to cater for them that the *Marion* was put on the loch. Likewise, in the last years, *Maid of the Loch* carried principally tourists and holidaymakers. In between, however, for almost a century from the 1840s until the 1930s Loch Lomond's steamer service was an integral part of the transport system of the district. It was how people got about. Not just people either – the steamers carried parcels, mails, even livestock. There were connections by coach and by rail. The first railway in the district, opened in 1850, linked Bowling, where the Clyde steamers from Glasgow called, with Balloch Pier whence steamers headed up Loch Lomond. Only later, in 1858, was this little railway connected into the main railway network. For a long period, from 1889 until 1969, the steamers themselves were railway-owned, and steamers connected with trains as an extension of the railway system. A passenger could buy a ticket from Glasgow Queen Street to Inversnaid as easily as one from Queen Street to Balloch – or, on board at the purser's office, *vice versa*. For many years the timetables offered a Saturday afternoon service to bring Saturday-to-Monday visitors from Glasgow to their lochside retreats, and an early morning Mondays-only one (6.30 a.m. from Ardlui) to return them to their offices in the city.

Nevertheless steamer services were much less frequent in winter than in summer, and what they had to offer the summer visitor was of greater importance. This was quite a lot, far more than the out-and-back, 'round the bay' type of excursion that is associated with trips on the water today. The steamers on Loch Lomond were a link in the vast network of tours by interconnecting trains, steamers and coaches which was available to the tourist in Victorian and Edwardian times, with connections not only to and from Glasgow but also Edinburgh, and the west and north Highlands.

Paddle steamers, although the most prominent, were far from being the only steam vessels on the loch. Steam lighters first developed on the Forth & Clyde Canal in the 1850s after the screw propeller became practicable, and developed into the off-shore Clyde Puffer of Para Handy fame. Steam lighters were used on Loch Lomond too, carrying mundane cargoes of slates and timber, and seldom, unfortunately, attracting the attention of photographers. Later in the century came small, privately owned steam launches to carry their owners about the loch. In this period too boating stations were set up on the banks of the River Leven at Balloch, half a mile below its outfall from the loch, to hire out rowing boats. From this it was a natural progression to offering trips by steam launch and, by the 1920s, motor launch. Private owners also took to motorboats rather than steam launches.

Although steam power on Loch Lomond goes back a long way, when it was first introduced the loch and the River Leven - which connects Loch Lomond with the Firth of Clyde - were already busy inland waterways. Over the centuries they had seen logboats, curraghs and rafts, Viking ships and naval pinnaces, galleys and birlinns, gabbarts and scows. Gabbarts were the sailing barges of the Clyde; those that came up the Leven, tracked by horses, were comparatively small, carrying 30 or 40 tons, and could lower their masts to pass under the bridges. The river was never easy to navigate. As befits the outlet from a hill region subject to intermittent but sometimes heavy rainfall, it suffered from low water levels in summer droughts, and strong currents in winter floods. It also wound its way round a succession of sharp bends. Successive schemes for improvement were still-born. The last of them, for a canal from Balloch to Bowling, was overtaken by events, that is to say by the construction of the railway already mentioned. Subsequently, use of the river inevitably declined, but nonetheless continued on a reduced scale.

The heyday of Loch Lomond's steamer services, from the late nineteenth century through to the mid-twentieth, coincided with the heyday of the picture postcard, and it is from postcards and other photographs of the period that the illustrations that follow are drawn. They offer a window onto the steamers at their most flourishing, and the world in which they flourished. Individual steamers operating during this period were, for the most part, the *Prince George*, the *Princess May*, and the *Prince Edward*. *Prince George* and *Princess May* were built in 1898/99 as sister ships (which does not help when attempting to identify them in a distant view!); *Prince Edward* followed in 1911. Earlier vessels of course overlapped them, and so did the last of the line, *Maid of the Loch*, built in 1953. Surprisingly, the *Princess Patricia*, which worked originally on the Thames estuary and was on the loch from 1914 to 1938, does not seem to have featured in postcards, perhaps because she was used mainly for short cruises from Balloch Pier out-and-back round the islands: since she seldom approached the piers up the loch, there would have been few opportunities for photographers.

The illustrations that follow are laid out in the order in which their locations were encountered by visitors. Some came only to Balloch, but many, probably most, travelled further up the loch by steamer, perhaps as far as the head of the loch and back again.

Paddle steamers for Loch Lomond were usually built on the Clyde and delivered via the River Leven. In the early days when steamers were small and the river was in regular use by gabbarts this seems to have caused few problems, but by the end of the nineteenth century steamers were getting progressively larger and the river seeing less and less use by large craft. Taking a steamer up the river meant doing so in the aftermath of heavy rain, which helped by providing the necessary depth although the strong currents the rain caused could be a hindrance. Horses towing from the bank supplemented the ships' own engines, but *Prince George* and *Princess May* both took several days to ascend the river. *Prince Edward* was larger and her construction was delayed by an industrial dispute and a fire at the builder's shipyard. When an attempt was made to take her up the river in May 1911, the water level fell and she became stranded until heavy rains came the following November. This photograph shows her on the last lap, over which she was assisted from the bank by two traction engines. She entered service the following year.

Coming up the River Leven, at Balloch there is still some three-quarters of a mile to go before Loch Lomond is reached, but the river there is broad, deep and readily navigable. Balloch Bridge is in the background. Close to the location of this view a barrage was built across the river in the late 1960s to maintain the level of the loch for extraction of drinking water. Slipways were built upstream and downstream of the barrage to enable small craft to be taken past it, and legal opinion has been expressed that the Leven remains a 'public navigable river'. If, as is now proposed, it is to be made fully navigable throughout, this is one of the places where a lock will be required.

Most tourists and holidaymakers heading for Loch Lomond came by train to Balloch over the line from Glasgow, Bowling and Dumbarton. This is Balloch Central Station where, since it was close to the Leven, they could alight for launch trips or to hire a dinghy. In those days the station was immediately north of the main road through the village, and this is the view from the level crossing looking towards Balloch Pier; half-a-mile further on, the station there was solely a point of interchange between trains and steamers so, allowing for the usual left-hand running, the parcels on the platform on the left were likely to be destined for one of the steamer piers up the loch.

There were two railways to bring visitors to Balloch: as well as the line from Dumbarton, the Forth & Clyde Junction Railway came across country from Stirling. Jamestown Station, seen here, was its last stop before Balloch Central. When this line was opened in 1856 it was Balloch's first link to the main railway system. Passenger trains were withdrawn as early as 1934 when competition from motor vehicles became serious.

Strictly speaking there were three rail routes to Balloch from 1908, when Dumbarton Burgh and County Tramways Ltd opened its line from Dalmuir and Dumbarton. This was an electric tramway, running along the roads even in country districts. It approached Balloch along the road from Alexandria, and the terminus was immediately west of the level crossing at Balloch Central Station. As many as 49,000 people are said to have travelled to Balloch by tramcar during the first weekend after the line was opened, but within twenty years motor buses had creamed off the traffic and the system closed in 1928.

It was only a short walk from Balloch Central Station and the tramway terminus to Balloch Bridge over the River Leven. Visitors wanting to go on a boat trip, or to hire a dinghy, headed down the slope to the left of the wall in the picture, perhaps pausing for an ice cream at the Loch Lomond Tea Rooms on the way.

Between the world wars the Leven north of Balloch Bridge was a broad and busy river. In earlier times the loch steamers had started from this point when there was enough water in the river. When there was not, passengers were taken in scows or small boats up the river to the loch where the steamer lay at anchor. These arrangements ceased in 1850 when Balloch Pier and the railway were opened. Eventually in the 1880s and 1890s Balloch Bridge became the base for rowing boat hire, and trips by steam launches; there were two principal operators - Lynn and Sweeney. Several tripping steam launches were based here. Eventually all were replaced by motor launches such as the one just leaving the jetty. It probably belonged to operator Henry Lynn.

Immediately upstream from Balloch Bridge the Leven is divided by Monkey Island and this view shows the eastern channel and the east bank of the river on a quiet day, with the main river and Loch Lomond in the distance. Houseboats such as those seen here and in the preceding picture became extremely popular in the 1920s. A count in 1925 found no less than 126 houseboats on the Leven at Balloch, occupied by around 350 people.

Several privately owned steam launches were based at Balloch, and the owner of one of them is using it to support a right-of-way demonstration on 12 August 1911 - public access to the banks of the river was a contentious issue at that time. This well-proportioned little vessel is a typical steam launch of the period, and could have come from any one of several builders. The 'tea boat' in the background was a floating café.

Viewed from the boating station on the west bank of the Leven by Balloch Bridge, a steam launch and an early motor launch lie at their moorings by the island. They may have been passenger trip vessels.

*Above*: A leisurely day on the river at Balloch - day visitors are in rowing boats, windows are open to air the interior of the houseboat and a steam launch, with awning, is lying on its mooring.

*Opposite*: The location here is the same as the above photograph, although the viewpoint is a few yards further across the bridge. Boats visible in both pictures show so many similarities (even to the dress of the houseboat occupants) as to suggest that the two pictures were taken on the same occasion.

14

Looking up the Leven from Balloch, this view probably dates from the 1890s, for houseboats and other vessels have yet to congregate in quantity. However, a steam launch is lying on its mooring in the centre of the photograph and there is another to the right of the picture. Regrettably, it is almost impossible to match names to boats from this period. Contemporary volumes of Lloyd's Register of Yachts list only two steam vessels on Loch Lomond: one is the *Violet*, owned by the Duke of Montrose, and the other the *Chère Amie*. This was built in 1884 by Willans & Robinson Ltd of Thames Ditton, with a six-cylinder, three-crank tandem compound engine, for Hugh Mair of Henley-on-Thames. But, under his ownership, her 'Port belonging to' is listed as 'Loch Lomond' from 1888 to 1902. She reappears in the register in 1913-15 owned by Charles M. Collins of Maryhill.

Passengers heading for the paddle steamers stayed on board the train past Balloch Central to arrive at Balloch Pier. Station and pier are seen here in the photograph, probably taken in the 1930s, with the loch beyond. The railway to Balloch Pier was built by the Caledonian & Dunbartonshire Railway, which was absorbed by the Edinburgh & Glasgow Railway in 1862; the E&GR was in turn amalgamated with the North British Railway three years later. In 1889 the NBR's associate, the North British Steam Packet Company, bought out the Lochlomond Steamboat Company, and the steamers passed, in effect, into railway ownership. But matters did not rest there: in 1896 the railway from Dumbarton to Balloch Pier, and the steamers too, were vested in the Dumbarton & Balloch Joint Line Committee. This was controlled jointly by the North British Railway and the Caledonian Railway. Elsewhere, the North British and the Caledonian were in bitter commercial competition; by this date they both had their own routes from Glasgow to Dumbarton, and the NBR probably accepted the joint line arrangement as a lesser evil, the likely alternative being construction by the Caledonian of a competing line to the loch shore and the establishment of its own fleet of steamers on Loch Lomond.

At the end of the line at Balloch Pier, trains ran alongside ships for easy interchange of passengers and parcels. A curiosity of the joint line was that on the railway the track was owned and operated jointly, but the Caledonian and the North British each ran their own trains; on the loch, the 'track' was a public navigation, but steamers were owned and operated jointly. In this picture the train is a Caledonian one from Glasgow Central Low Level; the steamer, the *Princess May*, one of the first to be built by the joint line committee. The steamers usually came alongside the pier going ahead, and left it going astern before turning to head up the loch. A view of a steamer alongside but heading up the loch is so unusual that it is possible it was arranged especially for the photographer.

This is the *Prince George*, the *Princess May's* sister ship, in the more common position alongside Balloch Pier; North British Railway wagons stand on the pier railway tracks behind her. Construction of the two ships was preceded by all the contention to be expected when two such unlikely allies acquire joint responsibility. Both railways operated their own steamer fleets on the Firth of Clyde, and had divergent policies on steamer design and construction. The Caledonian, new to Loch Lomond, expected increased traffic and wanted large ships with forced-draught boilers, compound engines and all modern improvements of the day, to be delivered in parts and erected on the loch shore; the North British, with long experience of the loch, wanted ships of type and size known to be satisfactory and easy to maintain away from shipyards – that meant ships of traditional type, and short enough at 165 feet to be brought up the River Leven with its many sharp bends. The two companies had to go to arbitration before the North British view prevailed. The two new ships were built, like their immediate predecessors, with natural draught haystack boilers, and two-cylinder simple-expansion diagonal engines.

## A Loch Lomond Barge

After the appearance of steam vessels on the loch and steam railways on the shore, the use of sailing craft to carry freight on Loch Lomond and the River Leven declined and eventually disappeared. Just how quickly and completely this happened seems now almost impossible to ascertain – it may be that after gabbarts ceased to use the River Leven, said to have been in the 1870s, they continued to carry freight on the loch, to and from the railhead at Balloch. This sloop-rigged gabbart appears to be under sail off Balloch Pier. Yet, remarkably, no crew are to be seen - Loch Lomond's version of the *Mary Celeste* perhaps!

A pony and trap and its driver awaiting the steamer at Balmaha Pier. Balmaha, on the eastern shore, was the first port of call for steamers on their way up the loch. The pier adjoins deep water a quarter-mile from the village it serves.

Waiting for the steamer with a motor car at Balmaha Pier. The long lifetime of the Loch Lomond steamer services overlapped the change from horse drawn to motor traffic on the roads, but establishment of motor bus services to the lochside villages resulted in suspension of the winter steamer service from 1933.

The *Prince Edward* approaching Balmaha Pier. In the distance beyond is Conic Hill which marks the Highland Boundary Fault line. Balmaha village can be seen on low ground to the right. The *Prince Edward* was 175 feet long – the *Prince George* and the *Princess May* were 165 feet 6 inches – and had a two–cylinder compound engine. All three had open bridges which offered little protection from the elements – remarkable, perhaps, for ships to operate in a region where wet, windy days seem as frequent as still, sunny ones – and, equally remarkably, the bridges were positioned just aft of the funnel which cannot have helped visibility.

The Duke of Montrose's steam yacht *Violet*, elegant with her clipper bow, counter stern and raked masts and funnel, was for a long time a well-known sight at her mooring in Balmaha. Lloyd's Register of Yachts recorded her as being 50 feet long, built by Matthew Paul & Co. of Dumbarton. She was listed from 1886 to 1893 but, unless more than one successive vessel is involved, lasted much longer than that. In 1894 when Walter McGregor died – he had been resident keeper of Inchmurrin island for more than forty years, a well-kent figure among users of the loch – the *Violet* was employed to tow a small boat carrying the deceased in his coffin to Balloch; the funeral party travelled in the *Violet* herself. At Balloch this waterborne cortège was met by a hearse to convey the coffin to Alexandria cemetery. The *Violet* is believed to have lasted until after the First World War.

Luss, on the western shore, was the next call after Balmaha for steamers heading north. In their progress up and down the loch, the steamers zigzagged to and fro, alternately calling at piers on the east and west shores. So it was as easy to travel from Balmaha to Luss as from Balmaha to Rowardennan and the steamer service bound the shorelines of the loch together like the lace in a shoe, in a manner scarcely to be imagined today when the loch presents a huge barrier to movement between the districts on either side. In this photograph it appears to be the *Prince George* which is calling at Luss, heading south, with Ben Lomond prominent beyond.

Back on the east side of the loch, a well-laden *Prince Edward* approaches Rowardennan Pier. Probably many of the passengers would have disembarked here to ascend Ben Lomond by the footpath which starts nearby. Others would have set out to walk north along the shore to Inversnaid, following the footpath which would later become part of the West Highland Way. Then, as now, the public road up the east side of Loch Lomond came to an end at Rowardennan. The steamer service enabled people to travel further north.

The *Prince George* leaving Rowardennan to head up the loch. Many of the passengers are doubtless enjoying lunch in the dining saloon, forward, while the bonnie banks slip past outside the large windows which the ship's inland voyage made practicable. The dining saloon extended across the full width of the hull. In 1901 lunch of soup, fish, joint (beef or lamb) and cheese was on offer for 2s. 6d. Earlier in the day there had been breakfast, with a choice of fish, ham and eggs, cold salmon, sweets, tea and coffee, all for 2s.; later there was tea, complete with fish, cold joints and sweets at 2s., or 'plain' (tea, bread and butter, and scones) for 1s. According to Duncan Graham's book *Sunset on the Clyde*, by 1954 inflation had brought the price of lunch on board the *Prince Edward* up to 6s. 6d. but it was still a good solid meal – soup, meat and two veg., and 'Scotch' trifle. In the dining saloon there were still crisp white tablecloths and cutlery engraved with the company crest; in the tea room, aft, cakes and sausage rolls appeared on tiered cakestands like those still occasionally to be found in those few Highland hotels which have totally escaped modernisation. With ships cruising at around 12 knots, the voyage from Balloch to the head of the loch at Ardlui took a couple of hours, so there was plenty of time for passengers to enjoy a leisurely meal.

The *Prince George* reaching the next calling point at Tarbet Pier. It was a disaster at Tarbet, in the early 1840s, which led to construction of the steamer piers around the loch. Previously, the steamers had anchored and passengers were taken to and from the shore in scows or small ferry boats. But at Tarbet an overcrowded boat capsized, and about eleven of the occupants were drowned. Subsequently, the Lochlomond Steamboat Company negotiated with the riparian landowners and their tenants for piers to be built at places where the steamers called. Although the piers were built at the instigation of the steamboat company, they were privately owned, and the pier dues demanded (even though small) from persons embarking or disembarking became a source of niggling annoyance. A guidebook of 1908 described them as 'utterly indefensible "pier dues" extracted from the traveller whenever he sets foot … on any one of the rough plank-and-pile structures which serve us as landing stages.'

Tarbet Pier. The ship, heading north, is the *Prince Consort*, which dated back to 1862 and lasted until 1899. Her funnel colours are those of the Lochlomond Steamboat Company, which dates the view to before the 1889 railway takeover. A horse drawn omnibus and a larger horse drawn vehicle are loading passengers. They may simply have been taking passengers and their luggage to the nearby hotel, but it is more likely that they are to make the two-mile journey across the isthmus to Arrochar Pier at the head of Loch Long, where Clyde steamers called. This was a recognised connection – most passengers simply walked between the two piers. The 'Three Lochs Tour' – covering Loch Long, Loch Goil and Loch Lomond – remained popular into the 1950s and was withdrawn only when Arrochar Pier closed in 1972.

Steam launch *Lomond* belonged to Lynn of Balloch. She was hired out and is seen here at Tarbet Isle, far from her base, which suggests a hire of several days' duration. Tantalisingly, little else seems to be known about her.

S.S. "Princess May," Loch Lomond

A well-laden *Princess May* looks fine enough, and it is to be hoped the writer of the card found her less crowded when he or she travelled aboard. The really interesting feature is the message written across the sky: 'train 1st; steamer 2nd; coach 3rd; steamer 4; coach 5; train 6; that's how we are going to Edinburgh today…Fares from Glasgow £2. 2. 4'. The writer had reached the second stage of the most famous tour of all, the Trossachs Tour - train from Glasgow to Balloch, Loch Lomond steamer to Inversnaid, coach to Stronachlachar, Loch Katrine steamer to Trossachs Pier, coach to either Callander or Aberfoyle, train to Edinburgh. It enabled tourists, in the course of a single day away from the cities, to sample the finest of Highland scenery and simultaneously, at a period when the works of Sir Walter Scott were familiar to all, to visit the settings for some of his best-known tales. It could be experienced in the reverse direction, or as a circular tour from one or other city or many other starting points, or incorporated into a wider tour of the Highlands. One ticket sufficed, with detachable coupons, and luggage could be sent on in advance. The Trossachs Tour is impossible today.

THE FOUR IN HAND COACHES AT INVERSNAID, LOCH LOMOND.

Tourists disembarking from the steamer at Inversnaid would find four-in-hand coaches waiting to carry them to Stronachlachar, complete with top-hatted drivers in scarlet coats. In this photograph the steamer is heading south, a reminder that tourists coming from the north and the west joined in the Trossachs Tour by taking the Loch Lomond steamer from Ardlui to Inversnaid. Clearly to be seen, above and beyond the passengers in the left-hand coach, is the 'fan', the set of boards, hinged at one end to the top of a post mounted on the deck, each of them inscribed with the name of a pier and displayed as appropriate to indicate the places to be served.

There are at least four coaches in this photograph, fully laden with passengers who have arrived by steamer, and they are ready to set out for Stronachlachar in convoy as soon as the photographer has finished. This coach service was still running in the 1930s and became a tourist attraction in its own right; when it was taken off at the end of the 1937 season, to be replaced by buses the following year, it had become the last horsedrawn coach service in Scotland. To judge by the styles of clothing, when this photograph was taken the coaches were nearing their end.

At the railway grouping of 1923 the joint owners of the steamers, the North British Railway and the Caledonian Railway, were absorbed respectively by the London & North Eastern Railway and the London, Midland & Scottish Railway – so joint ownership continued and lasted until railways were nationalised in 1948. One of the first actions of British Railways, the new owner, was to paint the hulls of the Loch Lomond steamers black, and it is in this guise that the *Princess May* is calling at Inversnaid around 1950.

The Lowlands left far behind, in this photograph the *Prince Edward* has reached the northern end of the route at Ardlui Pier. Ardlui Station on the West Highland Railway was close by; passengers heading north continued by train, while others made an out-by-train, return-by-steamer excursion from Glasgow.

No sign of crew or passengers, but here the *Prince George* is gently blowing off steam as she rests at Ardlui waiting for the next sailing south. Today this location is occupied by a busy marina.

Securely moored and with her fire banked up, but otherwise apparently deserted, the *Princess May* (or perhaps the *Prince George*) waits at Ardlui between turns of duty.

The River Falloch flows into the head of Loch Lomond, and since time immemorial scows and other craft ascended it for a mile or so to a landing place at Garabal. Early steamers likewise entered the river. Much of the traffic was destined for, or coming from, the vast Breadalbane estates to the north. These estates included a peninsula, between the main river and a tributary burn, just upstream from Garabal which itself was on Colquhoun property. In 1844 a short canal was completed on the peninsula, leading from the navigable river to a basin at Inverarnan. Here Breadalbane traffic could be landed or embarked without charge; the existing inn was improved, and coach services established, in connection with the steamers, as far afield as Fort William. But the Falloch was narrow, shallow and liable to silt up; by 1852 Ardlui Pier had been built (on Colquhoun land) and steamers gradually came to use it instead. About 1880, long after steamers had ceased going to Inverarnan, trustees for Colquhoun of Luss started to build a low-level suspension footbridge across the Falloch at its mouth, to connect lands the estate owned on both sides. The Earl of Breadalbane evidently still considered direct waterway access to Loch Lomond sufficiently important to seek an interdict to prevent obstruction of the navigation by this bridge, beneath which steamers could not have passed. He was successful and the bridge was never completed. The stone piers which had been built for it remained *in situ*, unused, and are seen here.

Edwardian passengers wait to go aboard a steamer – either the *Prince George* or the *Princess May* – at Ardlui. They may have arrived by the North British Railway from Fort William, for Ardlui Station is just behind the photographer; or they may have come from Oban by the Caledonian to Crianlarich, and thence by the coach connection to Ardlui which was still maintained for many years after the rival North British / West Highland line had been opened and served the two places.

On 31 July 1946 the *Princess May* (left) and the *Prince Edward* were both at Ardlui together. During and immediately after the Second World War, the two surviving steamers on Loch Lomond were exceptionally busy, carrying as many as 500,000 passengers a year, because other recreational opportunities were much curtailed. This photograph was evidently taken on one of the days when both were needed to carry heavy holiday traffic.

As with the *Princess May*, the *Prince Edward*'s hull was painted black by British Railways. It is therefore around 1950 that she is seen here at Ardlui. But she did not remain long in that form, for she was soon repainted again, to match the new arrival, the *Maid of the Loch*.

Last and largest of Loch Lomond's paddle steamers, the *Maid of the Loch* entered service in 1953. The wisdom of building so large a ship at that date has been questioned ever since, for over time she proved to be larger than needed for the amount of passengers available. Yet criticism is easy with the benefit of hindsight. After the Second World War, traffic declined, but it certainly did not collapse. Duncan Graham records that even as late as 1954 landing four to five hundred passengers at Tarbet, for the Three Lochs Tour, was 'not unusual'. And that was from the *Prince Edward*: simultaneously, the *Maid* was somewhere else on the loch with a whole lot more passengers. So it seems that, in 1950, British Railways had been faced with two elderly steamers on Loch Lomond needing urgent replacement, and had decided to build one big new one able to carry all the traffic. As soon as the *Maid of the Loch* arrived, the *Princess May* was withdrawn; the *Prince Edward* lasted for only two seasons more. Here the *Maid of the Loch*, on the right, and *Prince Edward* are both at Ardlui. They can seldom have both been there simultaneously, and one would like to know what the occasion was. Flags flying from the *Maid's* foremast appear to spell out 'Welcome'.

42

The *Princess May* calling at Inversnaid on her way south on a hot, still Edwardian summer's day.

A piper entertains passengers as they stroll towards Tarbet Pier to catch the *Prince Edward* on her way south in 1922.

With a sunny afternoon and a light breeze, this crowd going aboard the *Princess May* at Tarbet in 1913 could expect a pleasant sail down the loch.

Leaving Luss for the south, this steamer is probably the *Queen*, built in 1883. She plied her trade until 1911. Some schedules took steamers direct from Luss to Balloch, omitting a call at Balmaha. The famously attractive main street of Luss led down to the steamer pier which, in the great days, was an embellishment to it. By the late 1970s the pier, derelict, was rather less of an embellishment: 'sticking out like a sore thumb' was how the *Glasgow Herald* put it. During the post-war decades, owners of piers, which were made from timber, had become increasingly reluctant to maintain them as they made little, if any, revenue, and the large and heavy *Maid of the Loch* may have tended to cause damage when coming alongside. After successive closures, by 1977 only Rowardennan and Inversnaid were left for the *Maid* to call at up the loch. In 1978 the local authorities took a hand, and started a programme of rebuilding and re-opening the piers. This was too late for the *Maid of the Loch*; although she was able to call at Luss in 1980 and 1981, she was sold after that season and has yet to return to service. Her successor, the much more compact motor vessel the *Countess Fiona*, was able to take advantage of the re–opening of Tarbet Pier, but the service she provided up and down the loch lasted only until 1989. In the meantime the railway from Balloch Central to Balloch Pier was closed in 1986. Since 1989 the piers have been used only by local tripping craft and private boats.

Steamers taking the direct course south from Luss passed the entrance to Camstradden Bay; slate from quarries on the hillside was shipped from here, and a two-masted gabbart, probably used in connection with this trade, is lying on a mooring.

Not far south of Camstradden, steamers passed Swan Island and its little bay which, like the River Leven, was a popular mooring place for houseboats.